THE RISE OF TALIBAN AND THE SECRET OF HINDUKUSH

HOW A GROUP OF TALIBAN FIGHTERS DEFEATED USA

ISHWAR SINGH

Copyright © Ishwar Singh
All Rights Reserved.

I am dedicating this book to those innocents who lost their lives
during the war between insurgent groups of Afghanistan and the
United States of America.

Contents

Foreword   *vii*

Preface   *ix*

Acknowledgements   *xiii*

1. Introduction   1

2. Ussr Invasion On Afghanistan   3

3. How Ussr Lost The Game?   7

4. Formation Of Taliban And Its First Government   9

5. 9/11 Attack On Usa   11

6. Usa Sent Troops To Afghanistan   13

7. Role Of Hindukush Mountains As Saviour Of Taliban   17

8. Us Expenditure On Afghanistan   19

9. Us-taliban Peace Deal   21

10. Kabul Recaptured By Taliban   23

11. Taliban Formed The Government Second Time   25

Conclusion   27

Foreword

In this book, the author has tried to present an integral work studying one of the most critical periods of and a turning point in the **International Politics**. Being a mother of the author of this book, I knew the talents which my son have from his childhood. The way of expression used by the author in this book is excellent. I am very delightful to write the foreword of this book. The author has prepared alot for this book and expressed everything which he learnt from the study of **International Politics**.

I knew him from his early childhood activities. The author is very fond of writing during his childhood days. It was the incident of the year 2000, when he was in class 4. He first time in his life presented an excellent poetry written by him. His hyms were like a mature writer. Everyone in the family appreciated his writings including me and my husband because it was very impressive.

In academics, during the school days his favourite subject was Social Science. He has always deep interest in the **International Politics.** He oftenused to discuss the politics of Pakistan, Afghanistan, Sri Lanka, USA,UK and so many countries.

Preface

Dear Readers

The new generation of students does not know about the role of Taliban in the history of Afghanistan. With the demand from my students about the clarity of the issue, I wrote this book.

It gives me great pleasure to present before you the collection of my notes in the form of a book. In this book, I have tried to use very simple language, to justify my views honestly with my readers.

As you read the title of this book which is 'The Rise of Taliban and the Role of Hindukush' you can understand the motive of this book. This book talks about the struggle of Taliban to recapture the power and failure of United States of America.

I have tried to do research on disadvantages of some of our important democratic practices so that we can understand, where we are failing. I just want to explore some important points regarding the International Political System so that our future generations could know about importance of it.

I have tried to express my views in short words and just provide briefly explanation the various issues. This work is based on my preparation of civil services. I have tried to present my notes of civil services in a brief and simple manner.

The difficulties that the author faced in collecting material for this study, however, were manifold. One of the serious difficulties that he found himself confronted with was to find the state records closed to scrutiny.

The writer has no claims to a deeper study of the International Politics, still less to any research work. He just a casual reader and an occasional contributor of an odd article. In the present work he has merely pieced together the collection of his notes in the context of 'The Rise of Taliban and the Role of Hindukush'.

The main purpose of this book is to provide a foundation for a long term program of research on International Politics. Despite an apparent abundance of information about International Politics, the problems in International Politics persist.

It is true that at a certain stage in the life of those countries where the people are fighting to throw off the yoke of foreign domination, nationalism has its virtues. But in the world of today where the great majority of people are free, emphasis on nationalism is not conducive to the creation of an atmosphere necessary for international understanding and goodwill, without which a new international politics cannot emerge.

The United Nations is trying, no doubt, to create such an atmosphere. But the gap between the promise and the performance, between the preamble of the Charter and the politics of the big powers, is the dilemma of all those who are anxious to "save the succeeding generations from the scourge of war" and to create a world order which will guarantee human freedom, rule of law, equal opportunity and economic security.

Peace among nations, economic growth, social justice, science in the service of man, technology tempered by humanity-these are only ideals. They have not become a coherent philosophy or a plan of action, nor is it possible for them to do so in today's world of territorial nation states with divergent interests and ideologies where no effective system of world law exists.

What is needed is a revolutionary change in the minds of men. As stated in the constitution of UNESCO: " Since war begins in the minds of men, it is in the minds of men that defences of peace must be constructed."

The present book, which for certain unavoidable reasons took longer time than anticipated, is a modest effort in that direction. It is hoped that it will focus the attention of young students on the issues relating to the International politics.

This is all about the preface of my book 'The Rise of Taliban and the Role of Hindukush'. I think you will enjoy this book and engage yourself in a thorough reading.

Acknowledgements

Writing a book is harder than I thought and more rewarding than I could have ever imagined. None of this would have been possible without my best friend, my teacher, my best motivator, my beloved mother Amarjit Kaur. She was the first who inspired me for my goals and taught me various subjects and created my interest specially in Social Sciences. She stood by me during every struggle and all my successes. Whatever I had achieved in my life it is due to my mother.

I'm eternally grateful to my father Pal Singh, who took in an extra mouth to feed when he didn't have to. He taught me discipline, tough love, manners, respect, and so much more that has helped me succeed in life. I truly have no idea where I'd be if he hadn't given me a roof over my head whom I desperately needed at that age.

To my father-in-law Narinder Singh for their moral support during the up and downs in my life. He taught me how to live positive even in the worst situations by his sharing his personal experiances. He is the man who suggest me to write a book in your life because it will be your book by which you will be remembered in future.

To Dr. Davinder Singh, who took a chance on a twenty-nine-year-old kid and let him run his offices in Akal Academy, Baru Sahib, Himachal Pradesh. He never saw my age, my race, or my lack of formal education. He just saw a kid hungry to learn, hungry to grow, and hungry to succeed in teaching. He never stopped me; he only encouraged me.

Writing a book about the **'The Rise of Taliban and the Role of Hindukush'** is a surreal process. I'm forever indebted to Birinder Pal Kaur and Naginder Pal Singh for their editorial help, keen insight, and ongoing support in bringing my research to life. It is because of their efforts and encouragement that I have a legacy to pass on to my family where one didn't exist before.

To everyone at the Scribe Tribe who enables me to be the teacher of a organisation that I'm honoured to be a part of, thank you for letting me serve, for being a part of our amazing organisation, and for showing up every day and helping more authors turn their ideas into books.

To my younger brother, Hardeep Singh: for always being the person I could turn to during those dark and desperate years. He sustained me in ways that I never knew that I needed. Thank you for letting me know that you had nothing but great memories of me. So thankful to have you in my life.

To Himanshu Jena, Thakur Sandeep Singh, Yashpal Sharma for their motivational support during my book writing days. To Shashi Bala Minocha for giving their extraordinary support specially for good Preface writing.

Finally, to all those who have been a part of my getting there: Sukhbir Singh, Devinder Kumar Sharma, Sumeet Kaur, Rinkpal Singh, Iqbal Singh, Kulwinder Kaur, Surinder Singh, Amandeep Singh.

CHAPTER ONE

Introduction

Taliban is a very popular name now a days due to their control on Afghanistan. Afghanistan, the country which was facing political instability from last few decades is now seems to gain stable political structure in coming days and they will continue as a politically stable country forever. Why I am saying this? According to my understanding of Afghan politics, I am writing my opinions and future predictions on Afghanistan.

In the history of Afghanistan, there was a only one man who controlled Afghan territories very efficiently and Afghan never revolted against him. He was Hari Singh Nalwa. Hari Singh Nalwa was the millitary commander of the Maharaja Ranjit Singh. Maharaja Ranjit Singh was one of the greatest king of India who ruled over Punjab for 40 years. After Hari Singh Nalwa no one came who defeated Afghans in their homeland.

There was a "Battle of Saragarhi" which was fought between British Indian Army and the tribes of Afghanistan. This British Indian Army was represented by a group of 21 sikh soldiers who fought against the afghan tribals with bravery but lost the war. After this battle, the britishers never supposed to be have a any border dispute between Afghanistan and British India. I think there was assumption by britishers that they can never defeat Afghanistan so its good to stay away from any dispute with Afghanistan.

After so many years, when USSR was on peak, did a huge blunder by having a invasion on Afghanistan and lost the war. Same thing done by USA and their forces of were also defeated by today's Taliban. In every war these were also the Mountain ranges of Hindukush who protected the insurgent groups of Afghanistan for a long time.

Now a days Taliban is in news due to its extraordinary development in Afghanistan. On August 2021, Taliban succesfully siezed the control of almost all territories of Afghanistan. Taliban took control of the Government of Afghanistan and claimed that they will run the country according to the Islamic Sharia laws.

Before the rise of Taliban in Afghanistan on August 2021, the country was ruled Ashraf Ghani who was the democratically elected President of Afghanistan. But he left the country two days before the capture of Kabul by Talibani fighters.

Now the question is that why Taliban attacked on the democratically elected government in Afghanistan? Why there was a fear among the Afghani citizens from the presence of Talibani fighters? Why most of the women does not like to live in Afghanistan ruled by Taliban? Why USA withdraw its troops from Afghanistan? How an army of three lakh Afghanistani troops surrendered infront of fifty thousand Talibani fighters?

There are lots of questions like this. In this book I have tried to answer all these questions.

CHAPTER TWO

USSR Invasion on Afghanistan

After the world war II, there was the rise of two super powers in the world. One was USA and second was USSR. The cold war started between these two super powers after the end of world war II. The cold war means the war without weapons. The world was divided into three parts. First, the countries who supported USA like majority of western european countries. Second, the countries who supported USSR like most of the east european countries. Third, the countries who adopted Non Align Movement which means such countries will support neither USA nor USSR like India.

In this cold war, USA tried very hard to disintegrate USSR due to the fear of popularity of communism throughout the world. According to the USA, the ideology of communism can provide setback to the ideology of capitalism. On the other hand, USSR shared a long border with china and like India there were huge boundary disputes between USSR and China in 1970s. That means during those days China was also against the USSR due to their border issues. When USSR invaded Afghanistan, India supported USSR.

The Soviet–Afghan War (1979–1989) turned into a war in which rebel companies recognised together because the Mujahideen, in addition to smaller Marxist–Leninist–Maoist companies, fought a 9-yr guerrilla conflict towards the Democratic Republic of Afghanistan (DRA) and the Soviet Army during the 1980s, on the whole withinside the Afghan geographical region. The Mujahideen had been variously subsidized commonly via way of means of the United States, Pakistan, Iran, Saudi Arabia, China, and the United Kingdom. The rebel companies withinside the geographical region of Afghanistan had been referred to as Mujahideen. During those years, there has been no status quo of Taliban. But we are able to say that those rebel companies in Afghanistan together fashioned Taliban after the crumble of USSR. Between 6.5%–11.5% of Afghanistan's populace is envisioned to have perished withinside the war.

The conflict precipitated grave destruction in Afghanistan, and it has additionally been noted via way of means of pupils as a contributing element to the dissolution of the Soviet Union and the stop of the Cold War, in hindsight leaving a combined legacy to human beings in each territories. The foundations of the war had been laid via way of means of the Saur Revolution, a 1978 coup in which Afghanistan's communist birthday celebration took energy, starting up a sequence of radical modernization and land reforms. These reforms had been deeply unpopular many of the greater conventional rural populace and installed energy structures.

The repressive nature of the "Democratic Republic",which vigorously suppressed competition and done hundreds of political prisoners, brought about the upward thrust of anti-authorities armed companies; via way of means of April 1979, massive components of the us of a had been in open rebellion. The communist birthday birthday celebration itself skilled deep inner rivalries among the Khalqists and Parchamites; in September 1979, People's Democratic Party General Secretary Nur Mohammad Taraki turned into assassinated beneathneath orders of the second-in-command, Hafizullah Amin, which soured members of the family with the Soviet Union. With fears growing that Amin turned into making plans to exchange facets to the United States, the Soviet authorities, beneathneath chief Leonid Brezhnev, determined to installation the fortieth Army throughout the border on 24 December 1979.

When the Soviet arrived withinside the capital metropolis of Kabul, they killed the Hafizullah Amin and deployed their personal puppet on region oh Hafizilah Amin. In January 1980, overseas ministers from 34 international locations of the Organisation of Islamic Cooperation followed a decision demanding "the immediate, pressing and unconditional withdrawal of Soviet troops" from Afghanistan. The Organisation of Islamic Cooperation is an intergovernmental corporation based in 1969, including fifty seven member states.

The employer states that it is "the collective voice of the Muslim international" and works to "guard and defend the pastimes of the Muslim international withinside the spirit of selling worldwide peace and harmony". The worldwide network imposed severa sanctions and embargoes towards the Soviet Union, and the U.S. led a boycott of the 1980 Summer Olympics held in Moscow. The boycott and sanctions exacerbated Cold War tensions and enraged the Soviet authorities, which later led a revenge boycott of the 1984 Olympics held in Los Angeles.

The Soviets to begin with deliberate to steady cities and roads, stabilize the authorities beneathneath new chief Karmal, and withdraw inside six months or a year. But they had been met with fierce resistance from the guerillas and had problems on the tough bloodless Afghan terrain, ensuing in them being caught in a bloody conflict that lasted 9 years. By the mid-1980s, the Soviet contingent turned into multiplied to 108,800 and combating multiplied, however the army and diplomatic value of the conflict to the USA turned into high. By mid-1987 the Soviet Union, now beneathneath reformist chief General Secretary Mikhail Gorbachev, introduced it'd begin taking flight its forces after conferences with the Afghan authorities. The closing batch of the troops withdrawn via way of means of USSR on 1989 and that they left the battleground among the diverse rebel companies and the Afghan authorities.

CHAPTER THREE

How USSR lost the game?

Afghan insurgents started to acquire huge quantities of guide via aid, finance and navy schooling in neighbouring Pakistan with extensive assist from the US and United Kingdom. They had been additionally closely financed via way of means of China and the Arab monarchies withinside the Persian Gulf. As documented via way of means of the National Security Archive, "the Central Intelligence Agency (CIA) performed a extensive position in affirming U.S. affect in Afghanistan via way of means of investment navy operations designed to frustrate the Soviet invasion of Afghanistan. CIA covert motion labored via Pakistani intelligence offerings to attain Afghan revolt companies."

Soviet troops occupied the towns and principal arteries of communication, even as the Mujahideen waged guerrilla conflict in small companies working withinside the nearly eighty percentage of the us of a that turned into outdoor authorities and Soviet control, nearly completely being the rugged, mountainous terrain of the countryside.

CHAPTER FOUR

Formation of Taliban and Its first government

The Taliban emerged in September 1994 as one of the outstanding factions withinside the Afghan Civil War and in large part consisted of students from the Pashtun regions of southern Afghanistan who have been knowledgeable in conventional Islamic schools. Under the management of Mohammed Omar Mujahid, the motion unfold all through maximum of Afghanistan, moving strength farfar from the Mujahideen warlords. In 1996, the organization administered kind of three-quarters of the usa, and mounted the First Islamic Emirate of Afghanistan, with the Afghan capital transferred to Kandahar from Kabul.

Mohammad Najibullah Ahmadzai, was the then President of Afghanistan who was brutally killed by Taliban. He was publically executed and hanged. He was from the People's Democratic Party of Afghanistan. Taliban gradually took control of the most of the parts of Afghanistan. Taliban had also tried to make their influence in the major policy decisions of the country. As a result, they were successful to implement Sharia Law in Afghanistan.

The Taliban's authorities turned into hostile through the Northern Alliance militia, which seized components of northeast Afghanistan and in large part maintained worldwide reputation as a continuation of the intervening time Islamic State of Afghanistan. The Taliban held manipulate of maximum of the USA till being overthrown after america invasion of Afghanistan in December 2001. Subsequently, the Taliban released an insurgency to combat america–subsidized Karzai management and the NATO–led International Security Assistance Force (ISAF) withinside the War in Afghanistan.

CHAPTER FIVE

9/11 Attack on USA

Early at the morning of September eleven, 2001, 19 hijackers took manipulate of 4 industrial airliners (Boeing 757s and Boeing 767s) en course to California (3 of them headed to LAX in Los Angeles and one to SFO in San Francisco) after takeoffs from Logan International Airport in Boston, Massachusetts; Newark Liberty International Airport in Newark, New Jersey; and Washington Dulles International Airport in Loudoun and Fairfax counties in Virginia. Large planes with lengthy coast-to-coast flights had been decided on for hijacking due to the fact they could have extra fuel.

At 8:46 a.m., 5 hijackers crashed American Airlines Flight eleven into the northern facade of the World Trade Center's North Tower (1 WTC). At 9:03 a.m., every other 5 hijackers crashed United Airlines Flight a hundred seventy five into the South Tower's southern facade (2 WTC). Who became the mastermind of Sep 11 assaults on United States of America? Osama Bin weighted down became the mastermind of all this game. He became the chief of the Al-Qaeda, a terrorist group. He to begin with decided on Nawaf al-Hazmi and Khalid al-Mihdhar, each skilled jihadists who had fought in Bosnia. Hazmi and Mihdhar arrived withinside the United States in mid-January 2000. In early 2000, Hazmi and Mihdhar took flying classes in San Diego, California, however each spoke little English; finished poorly in flying classes; and ultimately served as secondary hijackers.

On December 27, 2001, a bin Laden video became released. In the video, he said: It has emerge as clean that the West in wellknown and America particularly have an unspeakable hatred for Islam. ... It is the hatred of crusaders. Terrorism in opposition to America merits to be praised as it became a reaction to injustice, geared toward forcing America to prevent its assist for Israel, which kills our people. ... We say that the give up of america is imminent, whether or not Bin Laden or his fans are alive or dead, for the awakening of the Muslim ummah (nation) has occurred. ... It is essential to hit the economic system (of america), that is the bottom of its army power...If the economic system is hit they'll emerge as reoccupied. — Osama bin Laden

The Sep 11 assaults ended in instant responses to the event, along with home reactions; closings and cancellations; hate crimes; Muslim-American responses to the event; worldwide responses to the attack; and army responses to the events. An good sized repayment software became quick set up via way of means of Congress withinside the aftermath to compensate the sufferers and households of sufferers of the Sep 11 assaults as well.

CHAPTER SIX

USA sent troops to Afghanistan

In 2001, the Defense Department did now no longer have a pre-present plan for an invasion of Afghanistan. Bush met together along with his cupboard at Camp David on September 15 for a battle making plans session. The army supplied 3 alternatives for army motion in Afghanistan: The first turned into a cruise missile strike, the second one turned into a mixed cruise missile and bombing marketing campaign lasting 3–10 days, and the 0.33 known as for cruise missile and bomber moves in addition to floor forces running interior Afghanistan. The CIA additionally supplied its battle plan, which concerned placing paramilitary groups to paintings with the Northern Alliance and, eventually, American Special Forces units.

Who have been the Northern Alliance? Northern Alliance turned into a army alliance of organizations that operated among overdue 1996 to 2001 after the Islamic Emirate of Afghanistan (Taliban) took over Kabul. The United Front turned into at the beginning assembled with the aid of using key leaders of the Islamic State of Afghanistan, in particular president Burhanuddin Rabbani and previous

Defense Minister Ahmad Shah Massoud. Initially it covered by and large Tajiks however with the aid of using 2000, leaders of different ethnic organizations had joined the Northern Alliance. This covered Karim Khalili, Abdul Rashid Dostum, Abdullah Abdullah, Mohammad Mohaqiq, Abdul Qadir, Asif Mohseni, Amrullah Saleh and others.

The Northern Alliance fought a shielding battle in opposition to the Taliban regime. They acquired assist from India, Iran, Russia, Tajikistan, Israel, Turkmenistan, United States and Uzbekistan, whilst the Taliban have been appreciably sponsored with the aid of using the Pakistan Army and Pakistan's Inter-Services Intelligence.

The invasion consisted of American, British, Canadian, and Australian forces, with different international locations presenting logistical assist. General Tommy Franks of US Central Command (CENTCOM) turned into the general commander for Operation Enduring Freedom. He led 4 challenge forces: the Combined Joint Special Operations Task Force (CJSOTF), Combined Joint Task Force Mountain (CJTF-Mountain), the Joint Interagency Task Force-Counterterrorism (JIATF-CT), and the Coalition Joint Civil-Military Operations Task Force (CJCMOTF).

On November 12, america tracked and killed al-Qaeda's range 3, Mohammed Atef, with an air strike in Kabul. The fall of Kabul began out a cascading disintegrate of Taliban positions. Within 24 hours, all Afghan provinces alongside the Iranian border had fallen, along with Herat. Local Pashtun commanders and warlords had took over at some stage in northeastern Afghanistan, along with Jalalabad; Taliban holdouts withinside the north fell again to the metropolis of Kunduz, whilst others retreated to their heartland in southeastern Afghanistan, round Kandahar. Hamid Karzai turned into the chief of the Pashtun Popalzai tribe and were an enemy of the Taliban considering that they assassinated his father in 1999. He had entered Afghanistan with 3 different guys on October 9, however turned into nearly killed with the aid of using the Taliban, and turned into extracted with the aid of using the CIA on November four.

This Hamid Karzai later have become the President of Afghanistan. During his reign, Government of India has supported the Afghan Government in exceptional ways. Government of India, built and proficient a parliament residence to the Afghan Government led with the aid of using President Hamid Karzai.

India's assist and collaboration extends to rebuilding of air links, energy vegetation and making an investment in fitness and training sectors in addition to assisting to teach Afghan civil servants, diplomats and police. India additionally seeks the improvement of deliver strains of electricity, oil and herbal gas. Also to offer Afghan college students scholarships.

On four June 2016, Prime Minister Narendra Modi and Afghanistan's President Ashraf Ghani officially inaugurated the $290-million Salma Dam with a capability of forty two MW energy generation. Water from the dam may even serve irrigation purposes. The dam is predicted to assist Afghanistan capitalize on possibilities to be able to open up as soon as the India sponsored Chabahar project, linking the port in Iran to Central Asia's street and railway networks, is completed.

Role of Hindukush Mountains as Saviour of Taliban

The HinduKush is an 800-kilometre-lengthy mountain variety in Central and South Asia to the west of the Himalayas. It stretches from primary and western Afghanistan into northwestern Pakistan and some distance southeastern Tajikistan. Most of the well populated Afghan villages had been settled near around the vast range of Hindukush mountains. So most of the Afghani people knew about the every secret locations the mountain range.

What happened with USA and how US army was failed to establish peace in the Afghanistan? Here is the answer. After the attack of 9/11 USA was in hurry to take revenge for the innocent peoples who died after the collapse of world trade centres. Osama Bin Laden, the mastermind of 9/11 attack was the main target of US security forces and USA was thinking that they should easily capture him from the Afghanistan. As we have discussed earlier, Taliban was running the government in Afghanistan, US forces started to attack on Taliban fighters. Very soon Taliban fighters left the Kabul and moved for the secret locations in the Hindukush range. They fought with US forces in different groups for consectively 20 years but could not defeated by them.

What strategy they had been adopted to fight with the US security forces? Taliban started to train his fighters in the secret caves of the Hindukush. Into that caves, they had been also started madrasas to teach their new fighters about the message of Quran. On the other hand USSR was supporting Taliban with advanced technology weapons to counter US security forces. From 2001 to 2021, George Bush, Barack Obama, Donald Trump and Joe Biden served as the Presidents of USA. But none of them were successful with their Afghan Policy to eliminate Taliban. Actually it was not possible for the USA troops to find out the Taliban fighters within the Hindukush in different caves. It was also not possible to do aerial bombardment on Hindukush ranges because they don't know the exact locations of the secret training centres within the Hindukush. In his media statement, Donald Trump told that it is very easy for USA to defeat Taliban, we will just throw some nuclear bombs on Afghanistan and the game will be over. But it would kill a number of innocent people of Afghanistan which America does not want to do.

CHAPTER EIGHT

US Expenditure on Afghanistan

According to the latest studies via way of means of the Brown University, USA, Through Fiscal Year 2022, the US federal authorities has spent and obligated $8 trillion greenbacks at the post-9-11 wars in Afghanistan, Pakistan, Iraq, and elsewhere. This determine includes: direct Congressional strugglefare appropriations; strugglefare-associated will increase to the Pentagon base budget; veterans care and disability; will increase withinside the native land safety budget; hobby bills on direct strugglefare borrowing; overseas help spending; and envisioned destiny duties for veterans' care.

At least 929,000 humans were killed via way of means of direct strugglefare violence in Iraq, Afghanistan, Syria, Yemen, and Pakistan. The quantity of humans who've been wounded or have fallen sick due to the conflicts is a long way higher, as is the quantity of civilians who've died in a roundabout way due to the destruction of hospitals and infrastructure and environmental contamination, amongst different strugglefare-associated problems.

According to the Brown University, the Current estimation for the expenditure at the Afghanistan from 2001 to 2021 is close to approximately 2.three trillion greenback that is little decrease than the dimensions of the Indian financial system. The length of Indian financial system these days reached at three trillion greenback. You can believe that how big quantity spent via way of means of USA on Afghanistan and were given nearly not anything in return.

CHAPTER NINE

US-Taliban Peace Deal

The Islamic Republic of Afghanistan, a member of the United Nations and diagnosed via way of means of america and the global network as a sovereign nation below global law, and america of America are dedicated to running collectively to attain a complete and sustainable peace settlement that ends the conflict in Afghanistan for the advantage of all Afghans and contributes to nearby balance and worldwide security.

A complete and sustainable peace settlement will encompass 4 components:

1) Ensures to save you the usage of Afghan soil via way of means of any global terrorist companies or people towards the safety of america and its allies.

2) A timeline for the withdrawal of all U.S. and Coalition forces from Afghanistan.

3) A political agreement as a result of intra-Afghan speak and negotiations among the Taliban and an inclusive negotiating crew of the Islamic Republic of Afghanistan.

4) A everlasting and complete ceasefire.

These 4 components are interrelated and interdependent. Pursuit of peace after lengthy years of combating displays the intention of all events who are looking for a sovereign, unified Afghanistan at peace with itself and its neighbors. Peace talks among officers from the Afghan nation and the Taliban commenced in September 2020 in Doha, Qatar, however there has been a upward thrust in civilian casualties after that.

During May and June 2021, almost 800 Afghan civilians have been killed and over 1,six hundred others wounded because of the attacks, the very best range for the ones 2 months because the United Nations commenced systematically documenting Afghan casualties in 2009. This US Taliban deal is likewise referred to as Doha Agreement. Negotiations have been achieved via way of means of each events on numerous problems however all of it failed while USA withdrawn its remaining batch of troops from Afghanistan and Taliban recaptured the capital metropolis of Kabul after 20 years.

Kabul Recaptured by Taliban

After the US-Taliban peace deal USA was very much assured that after leaving Afghanistan, the situation should be under control and democratically elected government will run the country. But it does not happened. In a media statement, Donald Trump said that Afghanistan Army has three lakh troops and on the other hand Taliban has just fifty to sixty thousand fighters. When we leave the Afghanistan then it would not be possible for Taliban to defeat the huge number of Afghan Army troops. This was the wrong predictions took by the then President of USA, Donal Trump. Afghanistan Army was also had a fear about the invasion of Taliban after the USA withdrawal of troops. When Taliban had started to capture the western provinces of Afghanistan, the Afghan Army surrendered on the way.

The First reason behind this might be the advanced weapons with the Taliban fighters. Second reason might be the ideological match of both sides. When Taliban fighters started their march towards Kabul, the sitting President of Afghanistan Ashraf Ghani left Afghanistan and flew away to Uzbekistan. Actually he was in a fear that the Taliban will do the same thing with me as they did with the Mohammad

Najibullah Ahmadzai. The Army general of Afghan Army was already knew the strength of Taliban Fighters so he act wisely and surrendered.

In mid 2021, the Taliban led a first-rate offensive in Afghanistan throughout the withdrawal of US troops from the country, which gave them manage of over 1/2 of of Afghanistan's 421 districts as of 23 July 2021. By mid-August 2021, the Taliban managed each predominant town in Afghanistan; following the close to seizure of the capital Kabul, the Taliban occupied the Presidential Palace after the incumbent President Ashraf Ghani fled Afghanistan to the United Arab Emirates.

CHAPTER ELEVEN

Taliban formed the government second time

The Taliban had "seized strength from a longtime authorities subsidized via way of means of a number of the world's best-geared up militaries"; and as an ideological rebel motion devoted to "bringing approximately a simply Islamic state" its victory has been as compared to that of the Chinese Communist Revolution in Nineteen Forties or Iranian Revolution of 1979, with their "sweeping" remake of society. However, as of 2021–2022, senior Taliban leaders have emphasised the "softness" in their revolution and the way they desired "right relations" with the United States, in discussions with American journalist Jon Lee Anderson.

Anderson notes that the Taliban's conflict towards any "graven images", so energetic of their early rule, has been abandoned, possibly made not possible via way of means of smartphones and Instagram. One nearby observer (Sayed Hamid Gailani) has argued the Taliban have now no longer killed "a lot" of human beings after returning to strength.

Women are visible out at the street, Zabihullah Mujahid (appearing Deputy Minister of Information and Culture) cited there are nonetheless ladies running in some of authorities ministries, and claimed that ladies may be allowed to wait secondary schooling whilst financial institution finances are unfrozen and the authorities can fund "separate" areas and transportation for them.

On the opposite hand, the Ministry of Women's Affairs has been closed and its constructing is the brand new domestic of Ministry for the Propagation of Virtue and the Prevention of Vice. According to Anderson, a few ladies nonetheless hired via way of means of the authorities are "being compelled to sign up at their jobs after which pass domestic, to created the phantasm of equity"; and the appointment of ethnic minorities has been disregarded via way of means of an "adviser to the Taliban" as tokenism.

Conclusion

At the end, I would like to conclude the reasons behind the victory of Taliban against USA. Firstly, the secret remote locations in the Hindukush mountains, where they raised their new militants by providing them military skills from their childhood. Secondly, the weaponary support of Russia to Taliban fighters just to take revenge from the USA when USSR was in the battleground of Afghanistan and they lost the war due to the support Central Intelligence Agency (CIA). Thirdly, the patience of Taliban leaders and fighters for twenty years in the war with USA. They continousely struggled under an effective leadership to defend their homeland.

www.ingramcontent.com/pod-product-compliance
Lightning Source LLC
Chambersburg PA
CBHW021151130726
47988CB00004B/1552